DATE DUE			

HOW DO I GROW?

Questions & Answers About the Human Body

By Robert Carola
Illustrated by Mel Crawford

Cover by Stuart Trotter

FOREST HOUSE ™

FOREST HOUSE ™

This 1990 School and Library Edition published by FOREST HOUSE PUBLISHING COMPANY, INC.
ISBN: 1-878363-14-X

First published in the United States as "How Do I Grow?" by Fisher-Price Division of the Quaker Oats Company, East Aurora, New York 14052

HOW DO I GROW?
Questions & Answers About the Human Body

By Robert Carola
Illustrated by Mel Crawford

Cover by Stuart Trotter

What are the different parts of my body?

Your body is separated into different parts that do different things. You have a stomach that helps you eat, drink, and go to the bathroom. You have lungs for breathing, and bones and muscles that help you to stand up straight and move around. You have a heart that pumps blood that carries food and air to all the different places in your body, and you have skin that holds all the parts together. And in charge of it all, is your brain. That's quite a body you've got there!

What does my brain do?

Your brain, which is very nicely protected inside your head, is like a special "control center." As well as thinking, it also helps you see, hear, talk, sleep, grow, and lots of other things. In one way or another, your brain takes care of almost everything your body does.

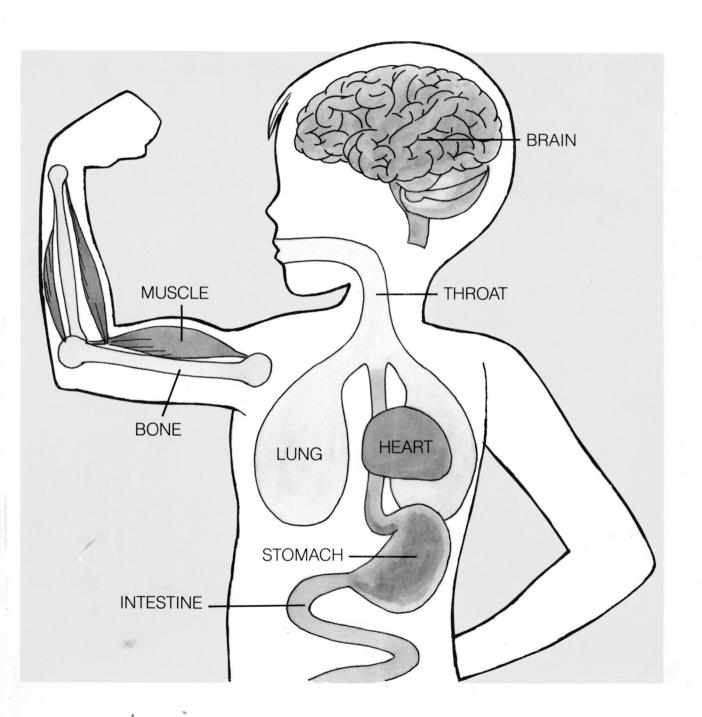

BRAIN

MUSCLE

THROAT

BONE

LUNG

HEART

STOMACH

INTESTINE

Why do I get hungry?

When you get hungry, it's your body's way of telling you that it needs a fresh supply of food. Your body uses food to get energy, to grow, to fix worn-out parts, and to do lots of other things that you don't even have to think about.

What happens to my food when I eat it?

Two things happen to your food when you eat it. First, it is chopped up into small pieces when you chew, and then it is churned up even more when it reaches your stomach. Special juices in your mouth and stomach also help to make small pieces. When all the food is mixed up and softened, it is pushed out of your stomach. Then, your blood carries it to the parts of your body that need it. When you go to the bathroom, you are getting rid of the parts of the food that your body doesn't need.

What happens when food "goes down the wrong way"?

Almost always, your food goes down a tube that leads to your stomach. The breathing tube next to the food tube is usually shut off while you swallow. But sometimes a little bit of food or water gets into the breathing tube—it "goes down the wrong way." When that happens, you begin to cough without even thinking about it, and before you know it, the breathing tube is clear, and you can get back to your meal.

Why do I get thirsty?

Your skin, muscles, blood and all the other parts of your body contain a lot of water. When you get thirsty it's your body's way of telling you that it's getting too dry. You get thirsty for lots of reasons. Maybe you haven't had a drink in a long time, or you ate some very dry food or salty food like potato chips. Or, perhaps you are thirsty from singing your favorite song for a long time without stopping.

Why do I burp?

When you swallow your food you may also swallow some air, especially if you eat too fast. That air has no place to go, so it comes up again, and you "burp." Sometimes you burp a little while *after* you eat, when gas comes up as you are digesting your meal. People usually think burping is rude— so it's nice to say "excuse me" after a loud burp!

What do my lips do?

Like your tongue, your lips help you to eat your food and to talk. Your lips can open and close to let food and air in, or they can close tight to keep water out when you go swimming. What are some other things you can do with your lips? Here are three: You can pucker up to whistle, you can blow out your birthday candles, and best of all, you can kiss your family goodnight. Lips are *really* important.

Why do my teeth have different shapes?

You have different kinds of teeth because they do different kinds of chewing. The sharp ones in front are called *incisors*. They are good for nibbling and tearing food like corn on the cob. The big flat teeth in the back, called *molars,* are used for crushing and grinding food like peanuts. You never even have to think about which ones to use. Your teeth just seem to know when to go into action!

Why do I have to brush my teeth?

You should brush your teeth after meals and at bedtime to wash away germs and the food that gets stuck between your teeth. Some of those germs can even use sugar to make your teeth sticky, so that *more* food sticks to your teeth! If you don't brush the food and germs away you might get cavities, little holes in your teeth that will have to be fixed by a dentist.

What do my fingers do?

Your fingers can do so many different things! The most important thing they do is to hold things. Because you have fingers you can draw with a crayon, hold a glass of milk, or imitate a crawling spider. You can also shake hands with your friends, throw a ball, or point at a beautiful butterfly. What else can your fingers do?

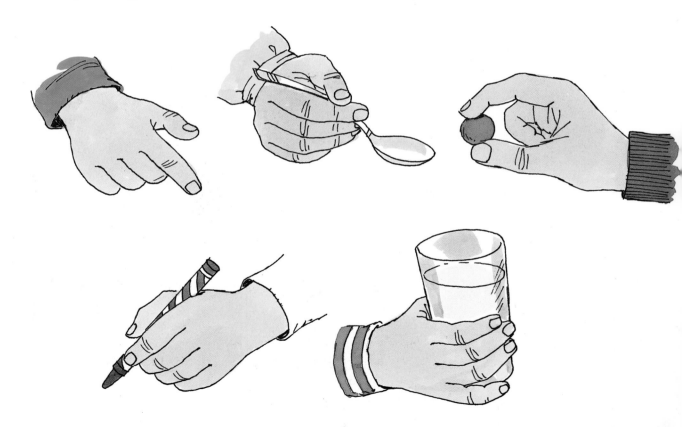

Why do my fingers look like raisins when I stay in the bathtub too long?

When you stay in the tub a long time, your fingerprints soak up a lot of water—just the way a paper towel picks up a spill. When you get out of the tub, the water in your fingertips leaks out through tiny little openings in your skin. Some of the water that was in your fingertips *before* you took a bath comes out too. So your fingertips look a little wrinkled for a while—just like raisins!

Why are my fingerprints different from anyone else's?

Your fingerprints (the tiny lines on your fingertips that you can hardly see) began to form even before you were born. There are so many different ways for the lines to loop and twist that there is no chance that your fingerprints will be exactly like anyone else's. Your toeprints, and the prints of the bottoms of your feet and palms of your hands are also different from anyone else's.

What do my toes do?

Because you have toes, you can stand up without falling over, and you can walk and run as fast as you do. And besides, toes are fun to wiggle in the sand!

Why do my shoes get too small?

Your shoes get too small because you are still growing. The muscles, bones, skin, and all the other parts of your feet (and the rest of you too) will probably keep growing until you are about 21 years old. But you do most of your growing while you are still a child. Sometimes you grow fast (like when you are a teenager), and other times you grow more slowly (like right now).

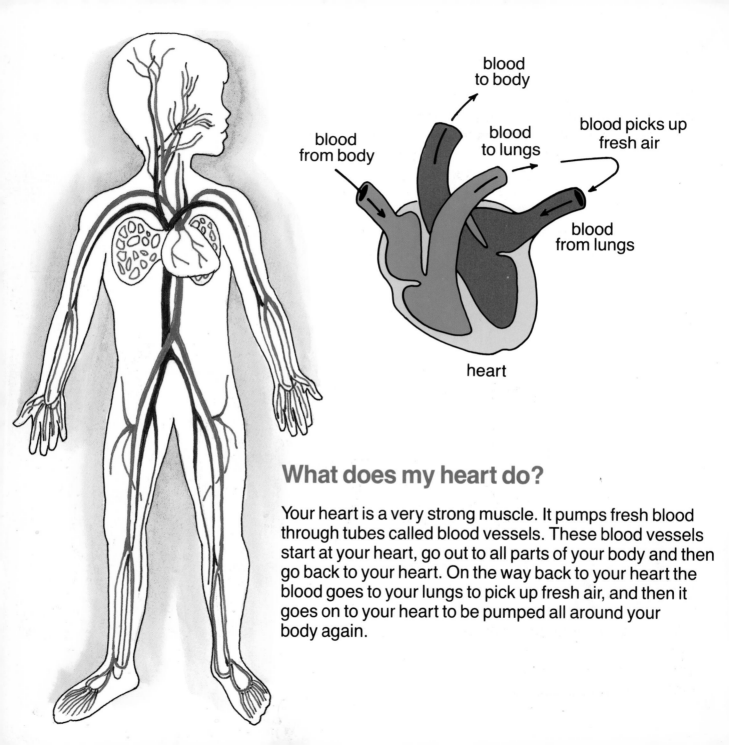

blood
to body

blood
from body

blood
to lungs

blood picks up
fresh air

blood
from lungs

heart

What does my heart do?

Your heart is a very strong muscle. It pumps fresh blood through tubes called blood vessels. These blood vessels start at your heart, go out to all parts of your body and then go back to your heart. On the way back to your heart the blood goes to your lungs to pick up fresh air, and then it goes on to your heart to be pumped all around your body again.

What does my blood do?

Blood does so many things that it's hard to tell about all of them. But here are some of the important things blood does. When you breathe in, your blood carries the fresh air to all the different parts of your body. While your blood is making the trip, it picks up the stale air in your body and carries it back to your lungs so you can breathe it out. Blood also carries little bits of digested food to all the parts of your body that need it. Blood helps to keep you from getting sick too. It has its own special parts called *antibodies* that keep germs from spreading. And these are just *some* of the things blood does!

Why does my heart beat faster when I run?

When you run, your muscles use up a lot of air in a hurry. You breathe faster to take in extra air. Then, your heart beats faster to send blood carrying that extra air to your muscles.

Why does blood look blue under the skin of my hands and wrists?

The blood you can see in the little tubes in your hands and wrists is on its way back to your heart and lungs to pick up some fresh air. Blood that isn't carrying much fresh air looks a little blue. Blood with a lot of fresh air looks red. That's why your lips and your cheeks look pink. The blood under the skin there has lots of fresh air in it.

Why does a small cut stop bleeding?

Special parts of your blood have a very important job. As soon as you start bleeding, they work together to make a plug that makes the bleeding stop. The plugging is called a *blood clot*. Sometimes, the clotted blood dries on your skin and makes a scab. Try not to pick at a scab—you may start bleeding all over again. Putting a bandage on a cut helps to close the cut and keeps germs from getting inside.

Why do I have hair?

Hair looks nice, especially when you wash and comb it, but most of all, hair protects you. The hair on your head helps keep you warm in the winter and cool in the summer. It also protects your head against bumps. Your eyebrows act like little cushions to protect your eyes, and they also cut down the glare of the sun and keep sweat from running into your eyes. Eyelashes are like little screens that keep dust and other things out of your eyes. How about the really tiny hairs on your arms and legs? Those hairs are too small to keep you warm or protect you from getting bumped, but they are really good at letting you know when a bug is crawling on you!

Why is some hair straight and some hair curly?

Each hair on your head comes out of a tiny opening in the skin of your head. A round opening makes the hair straight. An egg-shaped opening makes the hair wavy, and a wiggly-shaped opening makes curly hair. The kind of hair opening you have is passed on to you from your parents. What kind of hair do you have?

Why doesn't it hurt when I get my hair or nails cut?

The part of your hair and nails that shows is not alive, so there is no feeling when you get a haircut or trim your nails. The part that is alive is mostly under your skin.

Why do I shiver and get goose bumps?

Shivering and goose bumps are ways your body helps you to stay warm. When you get chilly, your brain sends a message to tiny muscles under your skin. Some of those muscles pull up the little hairs on your skin, causing small bumps. We call them goose bumps, since they look a little like a goose's skin. Your brain tells some other tiny muscles to just jiggle around a bit. All that jiggling makes you shiver. The jiggling muscles give off heat, and that helps you stay warm. Shivers and goose bumps don't work as well as a cup of hot chocolate, but they're a start!

Why do I sweat?

The purpose of sweating is to cool you off when you get too hot. Sweat is made in little compartments under your skin. When you get really hot, the sweat is sent up to your skin through tiny openings. Once the sweat gets on your skin, it begins to evaporate—it disappears into the air. But the sweat needs heat to evaporate. Where does the heat come from? From your skin! And, as your skin loses heat, you feel cooler.

Why are there different colors of skin?

Of course you know that paints come in different colors. The thing that gives paint its color is called pigment. Your skin has pigments, too. The dark pigment that gives your skin most of its color is called *melanin*. The more melanin there is, the darker your skin is. A yellow pigment called *carotene* also adds to the color of your skin. The thickness of your skin also has something to do with its color. Thin skin lets a little more of the reddish color of the blood underneath show through than thick skin does.

What does my skin do?

Your skin protects the inside of your body from dirt, germs, and other things you don't want to get in. It holds all your pieces together, and even gives you something to tickle and scratch.

Why do I have to wash my face?

If you look very closely, you can see that the skin on your face (and every place else on your body) has tiny openings called *pores* that look like little dots. It's very important to keep these openings clean by washing your face, otherwise they can get clogged up and cause skin problems such as pimples.

What do my bones do?

Bones hold up everything in your body and, because they are attached to your muscles, they also help you move. Without bones you couldn't even make a fist to knock on the door!

How many bones do I have?

When you were born, you had about 300 bones, but some of them are already joining together as you grow. By the time you are a grown-up you will have 206 bones.

What is my smallest bone?

Your smallest bone is inside your ear, along with two other ear bones almost as small. It is called the *stapes*. It is also called the *stirrup* because it is shaped like the stirrups you put your feet into when you ride a horse. These three tiny bones inside your ear help you hear.

Which is my longest bone?

Your thigh bone (the one that connects your knee to your hip) is your longest and strongest bone. It is called the *femur*.

What do muscles do?

Because your strong muscles are attached to your bones, they make your bones move. And when your bones move, *you* move too. It may be hard to believe, but you have over 600 muscles! Some are very small (the smallest ones are inside your ear), but they all help your bones to move so you can walk, run, jump, hop, twiddle your thumbs, and even hear!

Why do I hiccup?

There's a big muscle in your chest that helps you breathe. Sometimes that muscle gets tired and doesn't work as well as it should for a minute or two. When that happens, too much air goes into your chest, and a little trap door in your throat snaps shut to try to stop more air from coming in. The sound of the little door shutting and the extra air stopping is the noise we call a hiccup. Don't worry though, you'll stop hiccupping in a couple of minutes.

Why do I cough?

Sometimes you cough when you are sick and your throat is sore. Usually, though, a cough is your way of getting rid of something that's in your throat but doesn't belong there. If a piece of food gets stuck, or if little bits of dirt get into your throat, you blow them out by coughing. It's a good idea to cover your mouth so you won't cough on other people.

Why do I sneeze?

Sneezing is a lot like coughing. It can happen when you have a bad cold, but there are also other reasons why you sneeze. When dust, your cat's hair, or something like that gets in your nose, a special alarm goes off that makes your nose tickle—and guess what? You sneeze, "A-choo!" Bless you!

What is a fever?

When your mother takes your temperature by putting a thermometer in your mouth, she is trying to find out how hot the inside of your body is. Usually, if you are not sick, your temperature is about 98.6 degrees. If you're not feeling well, your body may be hotter than that. When that happens, we say you have a "fever." Usually, the higher your temperature is, the sicker you are. But, in a couple of days, your fever should go down and you will feel better.

Why do I yawn?

When you are tired you may not breathe as deeply as you usually do, so your body tries to make up for it by taking a big gulp of air all at once. *That's* a yawn. Don't forget to cover your mouth!

Why do I get tired?

You usually get tired when you play or work very hard, and your body needs some rest. You also get tired—or sleepy—when it's time to get to bed, so that your *whole body* can get some rest. You need lots of sleep to grow up healthy and strong, at least eight hours a night. If you get a good night's sleep, then you'll be able to play hard again tomorrow.

Why do I get out of breath?

You get out of breath when you play or work very hard, and you use up more air than you breathe in. You'll be fine once you stop to rest for a few minutes and slowly breathe in some fresh air.

What is an *allergy?*

For some reason, your body gets fooled by things in the air, like dust, or by certain foods. Your body acts as if those things could harm you and it sends out chemicals to protect you. These chemicals may make you act or feel funny—you might start to sneeze, get a rash, or have a runny nose for a little while. It means you are allergic to that particular thing. But allergies happen only once in a while. Most of the time your body knows exactly how to take care of itself every step of the way as you grow up. Isn't your body wonderful?